CONTENTS

FOREWORD

Ballet Dancing is a highly-skilled theatrical art which has developed during the past four centuries from the dances performed at the Courts of European Royalty. This book is not intended to instruct in the technique of ballet – in fact it cannot be too strongly stressed that the lessons must be taken with a teacher who is fully qualified in one of the reputable Dance Societies, otherwise untold harm can be done to young muscles, joints and bones. However, the child attending Ballet classes will derive benefit from this book since it will show her the full range of the technique which she is studying and will remind her of the correct basis of the exercises she is learning.

All children who learn ballet gain in grace and poise, even if they study for only a few years, since most children who attend classes have no intention of becoming professional. Although it is generally girls who study ballet, it can also be a help to boys both athletically and non-athletically inclined. To the latter it can give exercise without the rough and tumble of the sports field, and to the former it can increase ability by its development of controlled movement, co-ordination and self-discipline.

For anybody visiting the ballet, a knowledge and understanding of the subject must increase enjoyment and critical appreciation of the Art, and this book tries to give an insight into what makes a dancer.

Artistic Director—The Festival Ballet

LIST OF ILLUSTRATIONS

INTRODUCTION

This book shows all the basic movements in classical ballet and they are arranged approximately in the sequence of lessons usually followed.

Even the greatest dancers in the world practise the exercises and movements illustrated in this book. Pupils are always taken gradually through the various stages and you should not try to tackle the difficult movements too soon.

The book is not intended as an instruction manual – it is essential that you take lessons from a properly qualified teacher – but it will help you to remember the exercises you have learnt in class, and you can use it as a reference when practising or visiting the ballet.

Exercises start at the barre as this enables you to stretch your muscles and warm up whilst you are holding on to a support. Then, away from the barre, the same exercises are repeated using various arm movements to gain balance. This is known as 'centre practice'. After this come the slow sustained movements known as 'adage'; then the turns, called 'pirouettes'. This is followed by small and big jumps known as 'allegro'; and then beating the legs in the air, called 'batterie'. Finally, wearing pointe shoes, a girl will practise some of the earlier steps on full pointe, doing turns on the spot, and across and around the room.

Ballet as a theatrical art usually includes many other art forms such as choreography, music, costume, scenery and lighting, in addition to the dancing but these are not dealt with in this book.

Many of the words used are French and a list of the terms and their meaning is given on page 117.

Examinations

The Imperial Ballet Branch and the Cecchetti Society of the I.S.T.D., and R.A.D. all conduct or arrange Grade examinations for children who learn once or twice a week.

Major examinations are held for older children and students who wish to take up ballet as a career.

The Cecchetti Society also holds Class examinations which are especially helpful for children learning in educational schools and have only a short lesson once a week. These are taken as a class with the teacher giving the work to groups of six to eight children.

Practice dress

Girls

The usual practice dress for a ballet class consists of a simple tunic or leotard, with socks or tights and soft leather ballet shoes. Shoes must be bought to fit and not 'to allow for growing'. Ribbons should be sewn at each side of the shoe just behind the ankle bone. They should be tied neatly at the back and the ends tucked in.

The hair should be in a net, and held in position by a hair band.

Boys

The usual practice dress is a T-shirt, with black tights, white socks, and soft leather ballet shoes. These should be held on by elastic sewn on to the shoe just behind the ankle bone.

AT THE BARRE

First you will learn to stand correctly at the barre. The barre is a smooth length of wood fixed to the wall at a height comfortable to hold without raising your shoulders.

Stand far enough from the barre for the hand to rest lightly on it just in front of your body.

The weight of your body should be slightly forward over the balls of your feet, with your shoulders over your hips.

Most small children have "tummies" and they have to try very hard to brace these muscles so that the "seat" is relaxed down at the back and not "hitched up", so forcing out the rib cage.

Fig. 1. Standing correctly at the barre.

FOOT POSITIONS

There are five positions of the feet and all movements begin, end, or pass through one of these positions. In all positions the knees are straight and the legs are turned outwards from the hips.

The weight is evenly placed on each foot.

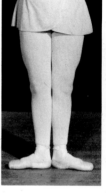

Fig. 2. Foot positions   *1st*   *2nd*

1st position. Heels touch. The aim is to make a straight line with the feet but this may not be possible at first.

2nd position. Heels about 12 inches apart, weight evenly on each foot.

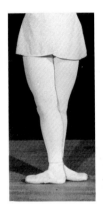   

3rd *4th opposite 1st* *4th opposite 5th* *5th*

3rd position. Feet are touching. Heel of right foot in front of hollow of left foot.

4th position opposite 1st. Right foot about 10 inches in front of left foot, with heels in line with each other.

4th position opposite 5th. Right foot about 10 inches in front of left foot with heel in line with toes.

5th position. Feet touching. Heel of right foot in front of left toe.

EXERCISES AT THE BARRE

Fig. 3. Plié (in the 1st position)

The Plié   Bend your knees sideways over your toes and move back to your original position. The movement is practised in all positions of the feet

and should be as smooth as possible.

You should go down until your thighs are horizontal. Your heels must be kept on the ground as long as possible (demi plié) and return again as soon as possible. In the 2nd and 4th open positions your heels remain down throughout.

Fig. 4. Battement tendu (en croix)

Battement tendu

Slide your foot along the floor from the 5th position until fully stretched in an open position (2nd or 4th). Then slide it back to the original position. The order of 4th (5th) 2nd

(5th) 4th is known as *en croix*.

If your foot remains in the open position it is known as a *dégagé*.

The movement can also be started from 1st or 3rd position.

Battement glissé or dégagé

This movement is similar to a battement tendu, but it is done more sharply and your foot should leave the floor.

Fig. 5. Rond de jambe à terre (*en dehors*)

Rond de jambe à terre

This is an exercise to turn out your leg in the hip joint. Your body and supporting leg should remain quite

still while your working leg moves in a circle, through 1st position, 4th front, 2nd position, 4th behind. The movement may be taken *en dehors* (away from your supporting leg) or *en dedans* (towards your supporting leg).

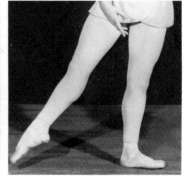

Fig. 6. Battement frappé

Battement frappé

This is an exercise to strengthen your leg and foot.

Frappé means "*strike*".

Relax your foot on the ankle in front, then strike the floor with the ball of your foot and finish in 2nd position.

Keeping your thigh still, bend the knee and bring your foot to the ankle behind.

Repeat the exercise, returning your foot to the original position.

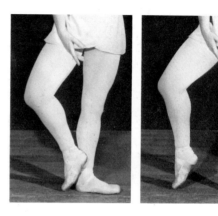

Fig. 7. Petit battement sur le cou de pied.

Petit battement sur le cou de pied

This is an exercise to help batterie in the centre, ie, away from the barre.

Place your foot on the ankle (le cou de pied) as in *battement frappé*. Keeping your thigh still and moving from the knee, open the foot to a small 2nd, and return it to the ankle at the back.
Open again to a small 2nd and return to the front of your ankle.

Fig. 8. Battement fondu (devant)

Battement fondu

This exercise helps you to achieve a soft and cushion-like landing as if on a trampoline.

Stand with your foot in a *dégagé* 2nd and raise it to 45°. Smoothly bring your foot under the supporting knee, which should bend at the same time. Gradually straighten, opening your working leg to 4th or 2nd with a feeling of resistance.

Rond de Jambe en l'air

For a single *ronde de jambe,* start with your leg in 2nd position at 45° *en l'air,* see fig. 8, 2nd photo. Keeping the thigh still, trace your foot through an elongated oval or triangle, coming in just behind the calf of your leg, passing to the front and returning to 2nd position. This is known as *rond de jambe en dehors.*

Fig. 9.

If the movement is reversed, ie, coming to the front of the calf first, it is known as *en dedans.*

Rond de jambe en l'air (*en dehors*)

For a double *rond de jambe* bring your foot in as for a single and open only half way to 2nd position, come in again and finish in 2nd.

Fig. 10. Grand battement (devant)

Grand battement

Your leg is "thrown" from 5th position to 4th or 2nd and returned to 5th. It passes through a *battement tendu* both on the way up and down.

Battement en Cloche

Based on a *grand battement*, your leg swings from front to back passing through 1st position and should be the same height in front as behind.

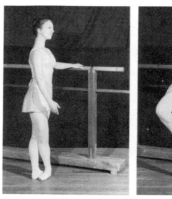

Fig. 11. Developpé (devant)

Developpé

From 5th position, your foot is drawn up to the knee (*retiré*) see fig. 11 second photo and

extended to 4th devant, held there and then closed again with straight knees.
The movement should be very smooth.
Repeat this exercise *en croix.*

croisé devant   *en face*   *croisé derrière*

Fig. 12. Directions of the body

CENTRE PRACTICE   After completing practice of all the
barre exercises, practise the same
exercises in the centre to develop

effacé
or *ouverte*

écarté

epaulé
or *ouverte derrière*

stability. They can be done facing straight to the front (*en face*) or facing in different directions.

ISTD >	*En avant*	*À la seconde*	*Bras croise*
C >	5th en avant		4th en avant
RAD >	1st position		3rd position

Fig. 13. Arm positions

ARM POSITIONS

The different methods of training call the basic arm positions by different names. We show those used by the Imperial Society of Teachers of Dancing, Cecchetti, and Royal Academy of Dancing methods.

Port de bras means "carriage of the arms". Your arms should move

Attitude	***Attitude greque***	***Bras bas***	***Couronne***	***Demi bras***
4th en haut		*5th en bas*	*5th en haut*	*Demi seconde*
4th position	4th crossed	Bras bas	5th position	Demi bras

smoothly between the various positions and you can at the same time transfer the weight from one foot to the other. At a later stage, your body also may be used in forward, backward or side bends, or a circular movement incorporating all these.

ADAGE

These are slow
sustained movements.

Fig. 14. Coupé over

Coupé

This movement is used to change weight from one foot to the other.

Dégagé right foot 4th devant with a *demi plié* or *fondu* on the supporting leg. Draw foot back to left foot and rise on *demi pointe*.

Change weight, lowering right heel and placing left foot on *cou de pied*.

A *"coupé over"* is shown in the photographs. When the movement is started with a *dégagé derrière* it is known as *"coupé under"*.

Chassé

This is a sliding movement of the foot forwards, backwards or sideways.

Start in 5th position and *demi plié*. Keeping *demi plié*, slide your foot into open position.

To recover and finish the movement, transfer weight, *dégagé* foot and close 5th.

Fig. 15. Chassé (en avant)

Arabesque

This is a position on one leg with the other extended behind—your arms should make diagonal lines with the palms turned down.

1st

Fig. 16. Arabesque

2nd

3rd

4th

5th

penchée

Fig. 17. Attitude

Fig. 18. Grand rond

Attitude

This is a position on one leg with the other raised behind: the knee is bent so that the thigh is higher than the foot. The arms are usually in 4th position.

Grand Rond de Jambe (en dehors)

de jambe (*en dehors*)

Dèveloppé leg 4th *devant*. Carry your leg through 2nd round to 4th *derrière*. Close 5th position.

The movement is shown *en dehors*. It may also be taken *en dedans,* starting with *dèveloppé* 4th *derrière,* through 2nd round to 4th *devant*.

PIROUETTES

These are turns on one leg with the other foot on the knee of the supporting leg. You can pirouette *en dehors* or *en dedans*.

En dehors. Prepare in 2nd, 4th or 5th with weight centrally between both feet. Your right arm is in front, the other to the side. Open the right arm slightly and join the left to it, at the same time raise your working foot and turn sharply towards it, rising on demi-pointe.

Fig. 19. (left) Pirouette (en dehors)

En dedans. Prepare in 4th with weight on your front foot with right arm across in front. Brush the back leg out to 2nd, opening your arms, then rise, bringing foot to knee, turning towards your supporting leg and joining the arms.

Fig. 20. Pirouette (en dedans)

Fig. 21. Fouettés rond de jambe en tournant

Fouettés rond de jambe en tournant

Usually known just as *fouettés*. The dancer makes a series of pirouettes remaining on one leg the whole time. Preparation is usually in 4th position as for *pirouette en dehors*—the dancer begins with a pirouette, lowers the supporting heel with demi-plié and extends the working leg to 4th *en l'air*, facing front. Continuing to turn, the dancer rises, whipping the working leg to 2nd position and again on to the knee. The arms follow the movement of the leg.

All these pirouettes call for quick turning, and the use of the head helps this. Keep your head to the front as long as possible, then turn it sharply to precede the body when facing front again.

All *pirouettes* and *fouettés rond de jambe* may be taken on the *pointe*.

Pirouettes can also be done in "open positions" such as 2nd *attitude* and *arabesque*. They are then done more slowly with the flowing quality of *adage*.

ALLEGRO This is the name given to small and big jumps.

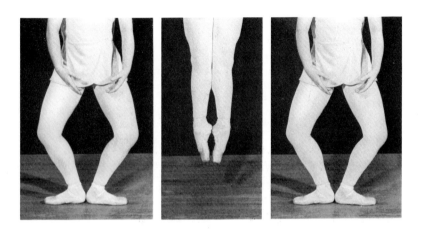

Fig. 22. Sauté

Sauté Although the word means to jump, it is usually applied only to those performed in 1st position.

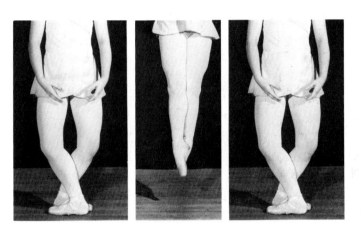

Fig. 23. Soubresaut

Soubresaut Spring in the air with your legs well crossed in 5th position.

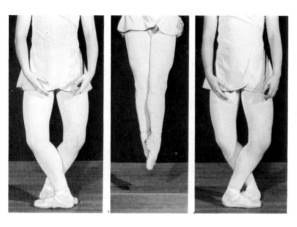

Fig. 24. Changement

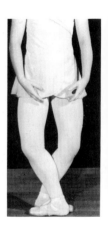

Fig. 25. Echappé

Changement

Start in 5th position, spring into the air, change
your legs and land with the other foot in front.

Echappé

Start in 5th position, spring and land in either 4th or 2nd – spring again and land in 5th.

Fig. 26. Temps levé

Temps levé

This is a spring or hop on one foot. The other leg may be in any position.

Fig. 27.
Glissade
devant

Glissade

This is started in 5th position and *demi plié.* *Dégagé* the front foot to 2nd; with a lilting movement transfer the weight and close the other foot behind. This is a *glissade devant.* The movement can also be performed *derrière* and *changé* (*changing feet*).

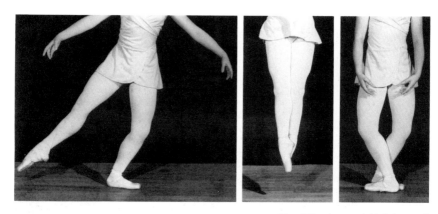

Fig. 28. Assemblé (devant)

Assemblé

Demi plié in 5th position. *Dégagé* the front foot to 2nd, spring into the air, join the feet together in 5th and alight. The movement can also be performed *derrièrre, dessus* (over), *dessous* (under) and travelling *en avant* and *en arrière* and *porté* (carried to the side).

JETÉS   A spring from one foot on to the other is called a *jeté* and there are many different types.

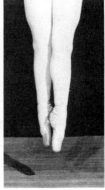

Fig. 29. Jeté ordinaire

Jeté ordinaire

From 5th position extend your left foot to 2nd, spring and alight with left foot on the *cou-de-pied*.

This may be done *derrière, devant,* also travelling *de côte* (sideways) and *en avant,* or *en arrière* with an extension to 4th.

Petit jeté

(*Not illustrated*)
Raise your right foot on to the *cou-de-pied derrière*, spring and alight on it with the left on the *cou-de-pied*.

This step can also be done *devant*.

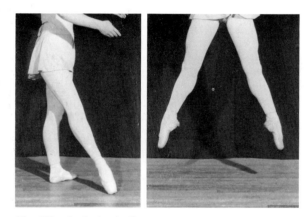

Fig. 30. Jetés by half turns

Jetés by half turns

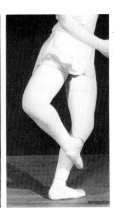

This is based on *petit jetés* or *jetés ordinaires* and taken diagonally, the movement is usually *devant*. The dancer always travels on the first half turn, but not necessarily on the second.

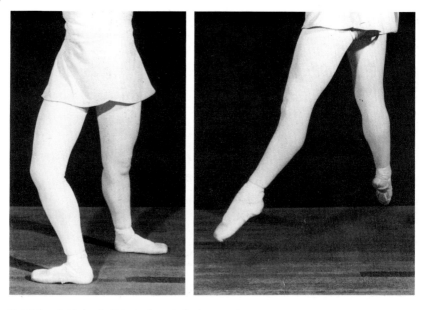

Fig. 31. Jeté by full turn (saut de basque)

Jeté by full turn (saut de basque) With the right foot, *glissade devant* and step to the corner.

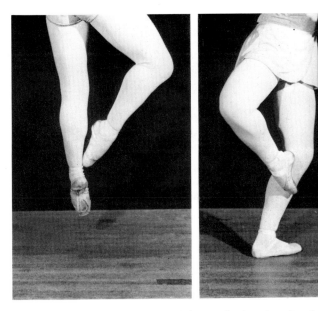

With a half turn throw the left leg to 2nd and spring into the air, taking both arms down and up to 5th (or *couronne*). Complete the turn and alight on left foot with right foot under the knee. The step may be taken across the room and in classical ballet it is often taken round the stage.

Grand jeté en tournant

Commence D.R. in 2nd *arabesque à terre* on right foot. With a running movement, step back on left foot, across and towards U.L. corner with right foot forward towards U.L. corner with left foot (*pas de boureé*) brush right leg forward and spring into the air taking arms down and up to 5th position (*or couronne*). Leaving right leg in the air, make a half turn to the left, change the legs at the back and land on the right foot with left leg extended behind and arms open in *demi bras*.

Fig. 32.

Grand jeté en tournant

Fig. 33. Jeté en avant

Jeté en avant

Brush the right leg forward – leap up and forward through the air landing on right foot with left leg extended behind. This is usually preceded by two or three running steps.

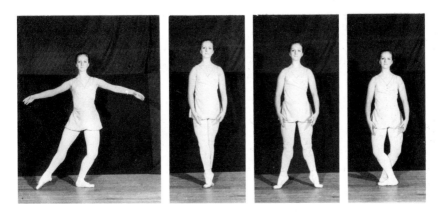

Fig. 34. Pas de bourrée (devant)

Pas de bourrée   *Dégagé* right foot to 2nd with
fondu on left. Draw legs together
rising on *demi-pointe*. Step left to
2nd, remaining on *demi-pointe,* close
right foot in 5th on *demi-plié*. The
step can be taken *devant, derrière,*
over and under, and turning.

Open pas de bourrée

Dégagé right foot to 2nd—step on to it on *demi-pointe,* join left foot in 5th, lower the supporting heel and either dégagé right foot to 2nd, or alternatively, place weight on it showing *demi plié* in 2nd.

The movement can also be taken *en avant* and *en arrière* using 4th position.

Fig. 35. Open pas de bourrée

alternative ending

Fig. 36. Pas de chat

Pas de chat   Stand in 5th position with your right foot behind. Raise your right foot with knee bent, spring into the air and bend up left leg, land on your right foot and close left foot in 5th *devant*.

Gargouillade (*Not illustrated*)

Stand in 5th position with right foot front. Raise right foot as in *pas de chat* and open it slightly to side—spring into the air making a small double *rond de jambe en l'air en dehors*—finish as for a *pas de chat* closing left foot in front. The second leg may make a *rond de jambe en dedans* before closing. The whole step may be started with the back foot and performed *en dedans*—then it does not change feet.

SISSONES

A sissone is a spring off two feet landing on one.

Sissone ordinaire

Spring from 5th position and alight raising one foot under the knee. The step is performed *devant, derrière* and *passé,* and *en tournant.*

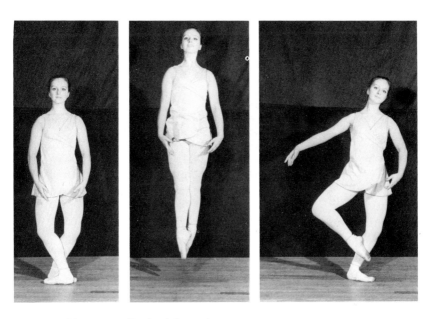

Fig. 37. Sissone ordinaire (*devant*)

Fig. 38. Sissone ouverte (en avant)

Sissone ouverte

Spring from 5th and alight with one leg extended.
The step is taken *en avant, en arrière,* and *de côté.*

Sissone fermée

As *ouverte,* but immediately after alighting, close in 5th position.

Sissone doublée

Consists of *sissone ouverte de côté,* a *coupé* and an *assemblé.*

Balloné (devant)

Fig. 39. Balloné (devant)

Stand on your left foot, with the right foot under the knee. *Temps levé* travelling forward, at the same extending your right leg, alight and bring the right foot under the knee again. The step is also taken *en arrière* and *de côté*.

Balloné composé

Perform a simple *balloné* (as above) but immediately extend the working leg again, step forward, *dégagé derrière* and close 5th. In the Cechetti method, the exercise is taken in 2nd as follows : *balloné, chassé* to 2nd, transfer weight and *coupé* under.

Fig. 40. Pas de basque (glissé)

Pas de basque (glissé)

Demi plié with your right foot in front, make half a *rond de jambe* to 2nd.

take weight on to the right foot, *chassé* through with the left foot, *dégagé* right foot *derrière*, and close to 5th.

The step can also be performed with a spring (*sauté*) or with straight legs (*grand pas de basque*). All can be taken *en arrière*.

Fig. 41. Ballotté

Ballotté

Stand on your left foot with right foot *dégagé derrière*. Spring and join both feet under your body, alight on your right foot with left leg extended.

Spring and join feet again. Alight on your left foot with right leg extended. This step is danced by Giselle and Albrecht in the first act of the ballet 'Giselle'.

Fig. 42. Demi contretemps

Demi contretemps This consists of a *temps levé* and a *chassé passé*.

Fig. 43. Full contretemps

Full contretemps   This consists of a *coupé* under, *chassé en avant* and a *demi contretemps*.

Fig. 44. Fouetté

Fouetté

This is a movement starting in 4th position, passing through 2nd position and finishing in arabesque.

Relevé on your left leg, brushing

the right leg through 4th to 2nd *en l'air*. Turn in the air to *arabesque* and land in this position. It is often preceded either by a *demi contretemps,* or a *pas de bourrée* as in *grand jeté en tournant*. The movement may be done by a spring instead of a *relevé*.

Tour en l'air

This movement is performed by male dancers, the step consists of a *changement* turning towards the front foot, either once or twice in the air.

Fig. 45. Tour en l'air

PETIT BATTERIE

This consists of the small steps of *allegro* performed with a beat at the base of the calf before landing.

Fig. 46.

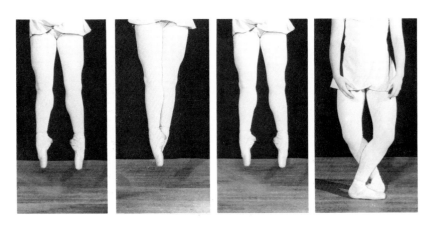

Changement battu

Changement battu Stand in 5th position and *demi-plié.* Spring into the air, slightly parting the legs, beat them at the base of the calf and land with the other foot in front.

Fig. 47. Entrechat trois

Entrechat trois

If the *changement battu* finishes on one foot it is known as an *entrechat trois*.

Fig. 48.

Entrechat quatre

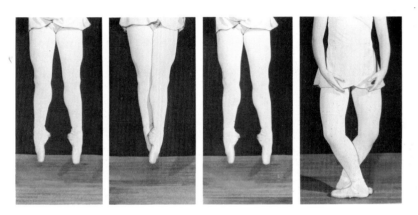

Entrechat quatre

Stand in 5th position and *demi plié* as for *changement battu*. Spring into the air and change the legs before beating and then change again before alighting. If the step finishes on one foot it is known as an *entrechat cinq*.

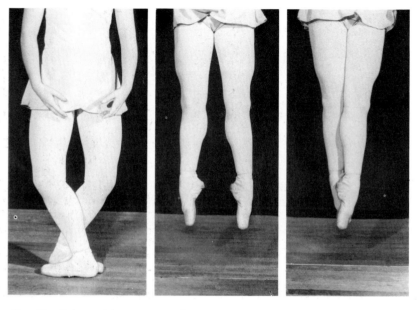

Fig. 49. Echappé battu

Echappé battu

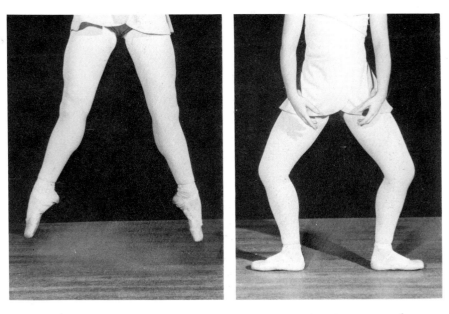

Taken to 2nd position. The beat to 2nd is that of *entrechat quatre*. Beat to 5th position may be either an *entrechat* or a *changement battu*.

Fig. 50. Brisé (over or dessus)

Brisé   Stand 5th position, right foot front, *demi plié. Dégagé* left foot to 2nd, spring into the air bringing the right leg up underneath the left to make the beat, change legs again and finish right foot front.

Fig. 50 shows a *brisé over*. It can also be performed *under, devant, derrière, en avant,* or *en arrière.* It may also be started or finished on one foot.

Jeté, assemblé, and pas de basque

All these basic steps may be performed with the beat of a *changement battu.*

Sissone battu

En avant, en arrière are performed with the beat of an *entrechat quatre. De côté* with the beat of either an *entrechat* or a *changement,* but more usually the former.

GRAND BATTERIE

This uses more elevation than *petit batterie* and the legs are more fully crossed.

Entrechat six

An *entrechat quatre* with an extra beat and therefore calling for more elevation.

Entrechat six de Côté

A *brisé over* with an extra beat and therefore calling for more elevation. The step is usually preceded by a *glissade* or a *demi-contretemps.*

Fig. 51. Brisé volé

Brisé Volé   Begin right foot dégagé 4th derrierè. Brush the leg through 1st position on a *demi plié,* spring and perform a *jeté battu devant* with straight legs. Brush the left leg back through 1st position and perform a *jeté battu derrière* with straight legs.

On the first part of the step the body tilts forward over the legs, and on the second tilts backwards – the arms may be used as wings to give the effect of flying. This step may be seen in the Bluebird variation from the last act of Sleeping Beauty.

Fig. 52. Cabriole devant

Cabriole devant Stand with right foot *dégagé* 4th *derrière*. Brush the right leg through 1st to 4th *en l'air* – spring into the air and beat the left leg up underneath the right leg.

Alight on left foot with a *grand battement* of the right leg. Close 5th. This step is usually preceded by a *demi contretemps* or a *glissade derrière*. The step can also be performed *derrière* or *de côté*.

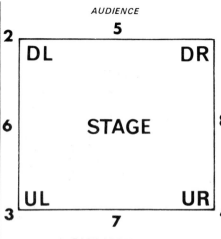

Fouetté battu

This is a *demi contretemps fouetté sauté*, performed with the beat of an open *cabriole devant,* and landing in *arabesque*.

The step can also be performed *en tournant* preceded by a *pas de bourrée*. The beat may be devant followed by the turn, or the turn may come first followed by a beat *derrière*.

Grand jeté battu

This consists of a *pas de bourrée grand jeté en tournant,* with *jeté battu derrière* after the turn and before alighting.

Directions as used on the stage

D = down   U = Up
R = right   L = Left

Numbers are used in the
Cecchetti Method

POINTE WORK

Pointe work should not be attempted until the bones have ossified (hardened), otherwise malformation of the feet may occur. It is also essential that the muscles in the pupil's back and legs are strong enough to enable the movements to be performed without strain and maintaining a correct stance. All steps should first of all be practised on the *demi pointe*.

Echappé

Start *demi plié* in 5th position. With a very slight spring open the legs to 2nd and alight on full *pointe*—with a slight spring return to 5th position. This can also be performed to 4th position.

Relevé

Relevé may be taken on two feet in any of the five positions. *Demi plié* and with a slight spring draw the legs under the body so that the toe takes the place of the heel, then with a slight spring return to original position.

This movement is also performed drawing the supporting leg under the body as previously explained and raising the working foot to the knee and returning to 5th position—it can be taken *devant*, *derrière* and *passé*.

Thirdly it can also be taken remaining on one leg. The supporting leg is again drawn under the body while the working leg is either extended to an open position, returning to a position under the knee, or held throughout in one position such as an *arabesque*.

Enchainement   *Fig. 53. Enchainement of echappé 2nd,*

An *enchainement* consists of two or more steps joined together.

relevé 5th, relevé devant, and relevé en avant

Fig. 54. Demi detourné

Demi detourné   *Relevé* in 5th, make a half turn towards back foot and lower with the other foot in front.

Fig. 55. Full detourné

Full detourné *Relevé* in 5th, but make a complete turn before lowering, with other foot in front.

Posé   A *posé* is a step in any direction and in any position. The most common *posés* are *posé coupé*, with the foot placed under the knee; *Posé developpé* with the foot passing through *retiré;* and *posé in arabesque.* The name is also given to a step on the flat of the foot, preceding a *temps levé.*

posé turn coupé   *lame duck*

Fig. 56. Enchainement of

Posé turns

These are based on *posé coupé*, but turning on the *posé*. This may be taken across or around the stage (*manege*) and performed *en dedans* or *en dehors*. When preformed *en dehors* they are often known as "lame ducks".

posé developpé　　　　　*posé arabesque*

posé turns and posés

Fig. 57. Petit pas de basque en tournant

Petit pas de basque en tournant

This is a step taken across or around stage. Spring on to right foot on *pointe,* starting to turn to right, sharply close left foot into 5th, *demi detourné* and lower immediately releasing right foot.

Fig. 58. Chaînes or petits tours

Chaînes or petits tours   The feet should be kept in 1st position and a half turn made on each step across the stage. The arms are held just in front of the body and the turns are taken as quickly as possible.

Fig. 59. Pas de bourrée pique

Pas de bourrée couru   This is a series of little running steps in 5th position – the knees are slightly relaxed and the back leg should move first so that a good 5th position is maintained. The steps should be quick and the whole movement travels as much as possible using a varied *port de bras.*

Pas de bourrée pique   Similar to that explained in *allegro* section see page 62, but the feet are picked up to the knee.

Fig. 60. Rond de jambe relevé

Rond de jambe relevé Stand in 5th, right foot behind. *Relevé* on left foot with right leg in 2nd, single or double *rond de jambe*, close right foot front. The step is often preceded by a *glissade* and may also be taken *sauté*.

Fouetté relevé As taken in *allegro* section see page 76.

Fig. 61. Enchainement

Developpé a la seconde

DOUBLE WORK

The highlight of all classical ballets is the *grand pas de deux* performed by the ballerina and her cavalier. This consists of an *entrée,* a supported *adage*, solos for the dancers and a coda in which the excitement is built up with jumps and beats from the man, and turns from the girl.

Developpé attitude devant

*Fouetté to attitude
derrière*

For his part, the "cavalier" must remember that his first duty is to show off the ballerina and that when holding her he must avoid digging his fingers into her flesh and so bruising her.

The hands are therefore held as flat as possible with the fingers in front of the body and the thumb behind. He also has to judge how close to the girl he must stand to keep her on balance.

*Promenade finishing in
arabesque penchée*

The following section deals with the supported *adage*.

It is essential that the girl should be so well placed that she needs little support from her partner — he is not there for her to lean on!

Fig. 62. Pirouette

Pirouette   For the preparation, the girl does a little *couru* forward and lowers into a *demi plié* in 4th – the boys hands are lightly on her waist. When she turns, the arms are crossed on her chest with the

elbows down so that there is no chance of her hitting her partner. The boy uses his right hand to help give extra impetus to the right, the girl turns inside his left arm, then he uses his right hand to control the end of the *pirouette.*

Fig. 63

Fouetté rond de jambe en tournant

The girl stands on *pointe* in 5th position, the fingers
of her raised arm are curled round the index finger of
the boy, her hand is holding his out in 2nd position.
She makes a *developpé* 4th devant with the right leg

Fouetté rond de jambe en tournant finishing in arabesque

then pressing with her left hand to give extra impetus, a *fouetté* en *tournant* with the left hand across chest. At the end of the turn she takes the boy's left hand again. As long as the girl holds her back firmly, the boy can help her to increase the number of the turns performed.

Shoulder lift

The simplest lift is on to the shoulder. The preparation is an *assemblé* during which the boy bends his knees to get his body under the girl — then using first his body weight and then his arms he lifts the girl up and back over the right shoulder and seats her on it. The girl must lift herself as much as possible, and then bends her left knee up with the right leg over it in *attitude devant*.

Fig. 64. Shoulder lift

Arabesque   *pirouette*

Fish dive   A position in which the boy lunges and the girl takes an
arabesque penchée with the underneath leg bent and the top
one straight.

Fig. 65.

fish dive

This series of movements is seen in many classical ballets

Bluebird lift

The girl makes a *pas de bourrée grand jeté en tournant* – as she steps, the boy kneels and places his right shoulder under her body and as she jumps he rises up. This lift is seen in the Bluebird *pas de deux* from "Sleeping Beauty".

It will be seen from these descriptions that complete co-ordination and sympathy between the partners are essential and are gained only with time and practice.

Fig. 66. Bluebird lift

Some French terms used in Ballet

Adage A slow carefully-controlled type of movement.

en l'air In the air.

Allegro A cheerful, brisk type of movement.

Arabesque A Moorish design. A pose in which the dancer stands on one leg with the other raised behind.

en arrière Backwards.

Assemblé To join together. A leap in the air, bringing feet together before alighting.

Attitude A standing position (see page 40).

en avant Forwards.

Balloné A bouncing step. With one foot raised to the other knee, the dancer springs up, straightening and bending raised leg.

Ballotté To toss. The dancer springs on one foot, tossing the other leg in the air.

Bas Down.

Batterie A jump where the dancer beats the calves together.

Battement A beating movement.

Battu Beaten.

Bras Arm.

Brisé To break. The dancer jumps from one foot, beats legs together and lands on both feet.

Cabriole To caper. A step where one leg is beaten against the other in mid-air.

Changé, changement Changing the position of the feet.

Chassé A sliding step.

Chaînés A series of small turning steps. *continued overleaf*

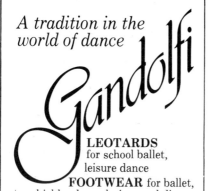
Cinque Five.

Cloche Bell.

Contretemps In syncopation against the time.

de côté Sideways.

Cou de pied Ankle joint.

Coupé Cut.

en couronne A crown. Where th arms are held in a curve above th head.

Couru Running.

Croisé Crossed. Where the dancer body is placed obliquely toward the audience.

en dedans Inwards.

Dégagé To disengage the foot from closed to an open position.

en dehors Outwards.

Demi Half.

Derrière Behind.

Dessous Under.

Dessus Over.

Detourné Turned away.

Deux Two.

Devant In front.

Developpé An unfolding of the leg.

Ecarté Separated.

Echappé An escaping of the feet from each other.

Effacé Where the dancer's body is placed obliquely from the audience.

Elancé To dart.

Entrechat (from the Italian *intrecciare* —to weave). A vertical jump where the calves beat together and feet change position.

Epaulé, epaulement The shoulders are turned at an angle to the hips.

Fondu Melting. A *plié* on one leg.

Fouetté To whip.

Frappé To strike.

Gargouillade A gurgle.

Glissade A slow, sliding step.

Glissé To slide, allowing foot to leave the floor.

Grand Big.

Greque Greek.

en haut Up.

Jambe Leg.

Jeté Thrown. The basic jump from one leg to the other, the first leg usually being 'thrown'.

Levé Lifted.

en manège Travelling right round the stage.

Ouverte Open.

Pas de basque A step of the Basque country. A circular swaying movement.

Pas de bourrée To hustle. A step where the weight is transferred quickly from one foot to the other.

Pas de chat A cat-like step.

Petit Small.

Penché To tilt. On one leg with the other leg raised.

Pied Foot.

Pique To prick. A sharp movement of the foot.

Plié Bend. A bending of the knees over the toes.

Porté Carried. A movement carried through the air, usually to the side.

Port de bras Graceful carriage of the arms.

Posé To place. A step.

Quatre Four.

Relevé To rise up on the toes.

Retiré The drawing up of one foot to touch the other leg with pointed toe.

Rond de jambe Circling the leg.

Saut, sauté A simple jump.

Seconde Second.

Sissone A simple step of elevation.

Soubresaut A jump with the feet in 5th position.

Temps levé A small jump where weight is not transferred.

Tendu Stretched.

à terre On the ground.

Tour, tournant. Turning.

Trois Three.

Volé Flying.